First Picture Dictionary
Animals
Premier dictionnaire illustré
Animaux

Pig
Cochon

Rabbit
Lapin

Butterfly
Papillon

Fox
Renard

Illustrated by Anna Ivanir

www.kidkiddos.com
Copyright ©2024 by KidKiddos Books Ltd.
support@kidkiddos.com

All rights reserved. No part of this book may be reproduced in any form or by any electronic or mechanical means, including information storage and retrieval systems, without written permission from the publisher, except in the case of a reviewer, who may quote brief passages embodied in critical articles or in a review.
First edition, 2025

Library and Archives Canada Cataloguing in Publication
First Picture Dictionary - Animals (English French Bilingual edition)
ISBN: 978-1-83416-294-2 paperback
ISBN: 978-1-83416-295-9 hardcover
ISBN: 978-1-83416-293-5 eBook

Wild Animals
Animaux sauvages

Lion
Lion

Tiger
Tigre

Giraffe
Girafe

✦ A giraffe is the tallest animal on land.
✦ *La girafe est l'animal terrestre le plus grand.*

Elephant
Éléphant

Monkey
Singe

Wild Animals
Animaux sauvages

Hippopotamus
Hippopotame

Panda
Panda

Fox
Renard

Rhino
Rhinocéros

Deer
Cerf

Moose
Élan

Wolf
Loup

✦A moose is a great swimmer and can dive underwater to eat plants!

✦*Un élan est un excellent nageur et peut plonger sous l'eau pour manger des plantes !*

Squirrel
Écureuil

Koala
Koala

✦A squirrel hides nuts for winter, but sometimes forgets where it put them!

✦*Un écureuil cache des noisettes pour l'hiver, mais il oublie parfois où il les a mises !*

Gorilla
Gorille

Pets
Animaux de compagnie

Canary
Canari

✦ A frog can breathe through its skin as well as its lungs!
✦ *Une grenouille peut respirer par sa peau ainsi que par ses poumons !*

Guinea Pig
Cochon d'Inde

Frog
Grenouille

Hamster
Hamster

Goldfish
Poisson rouge

Dog
Chien

◆ Some parrots can copy words and even laugh like a human!
◆ *Certains perroquets peuvent répéter des mots et même rire comme un humain !*

Parrot
Perroquet

Cat
Chat

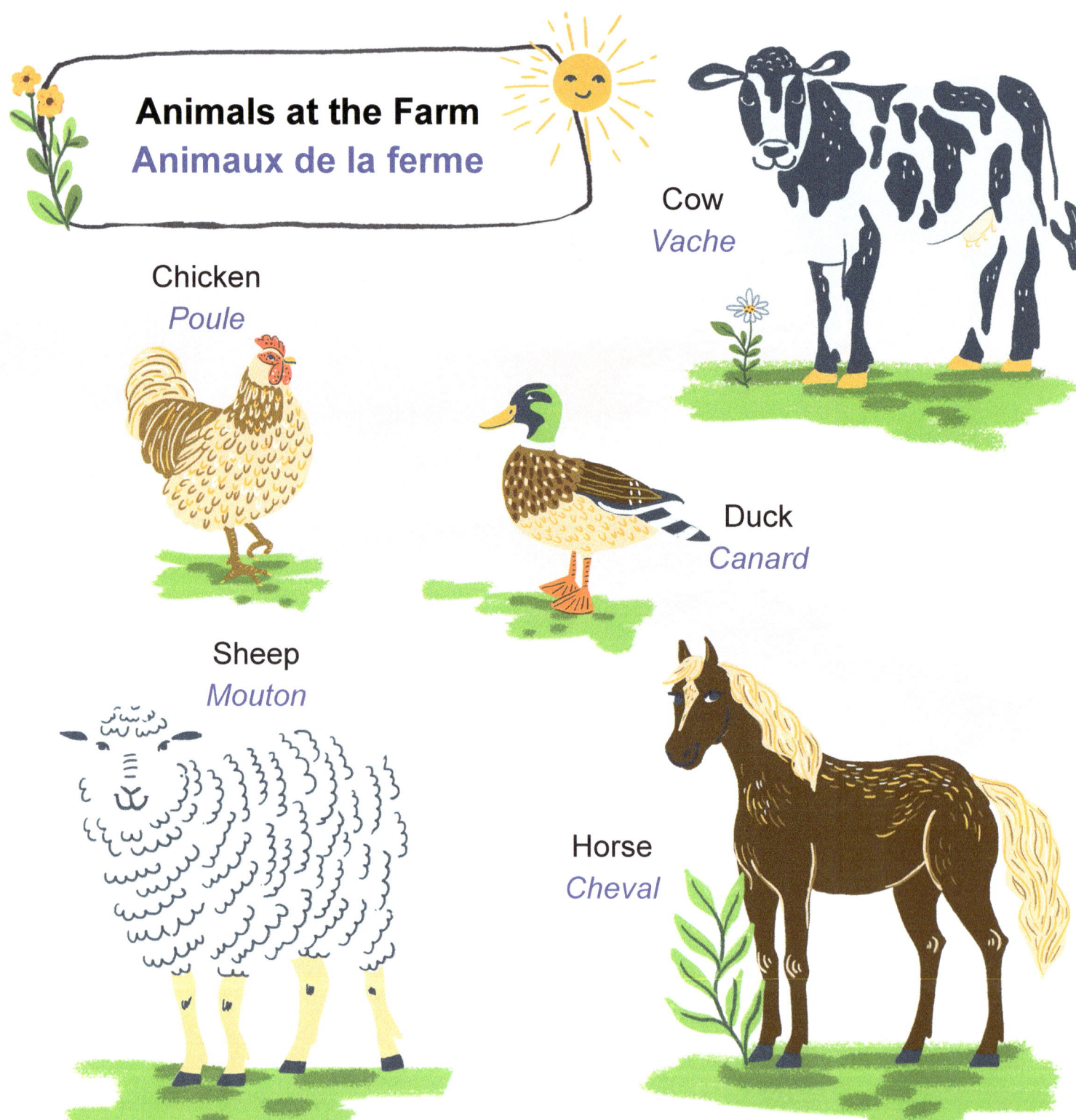

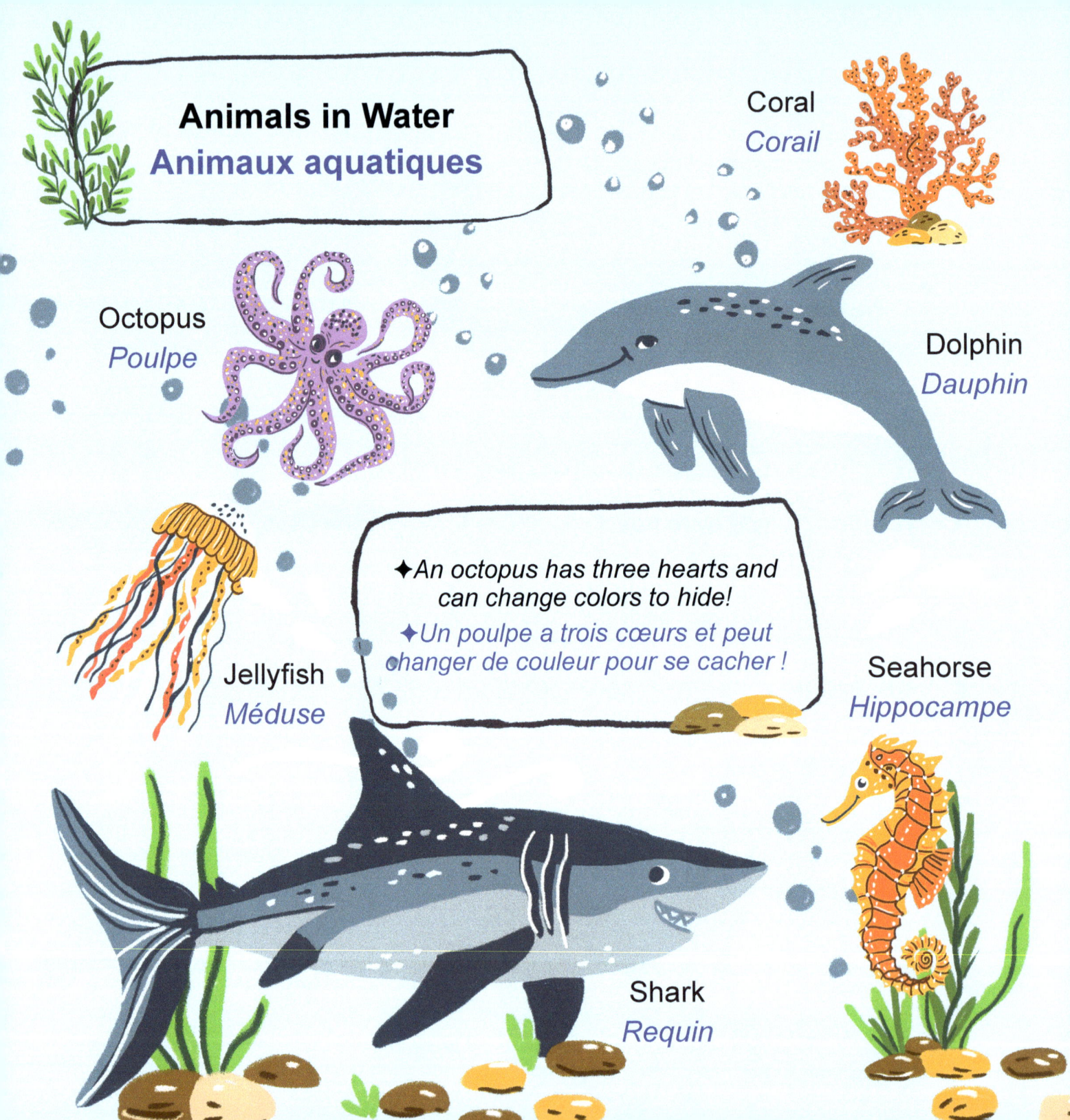

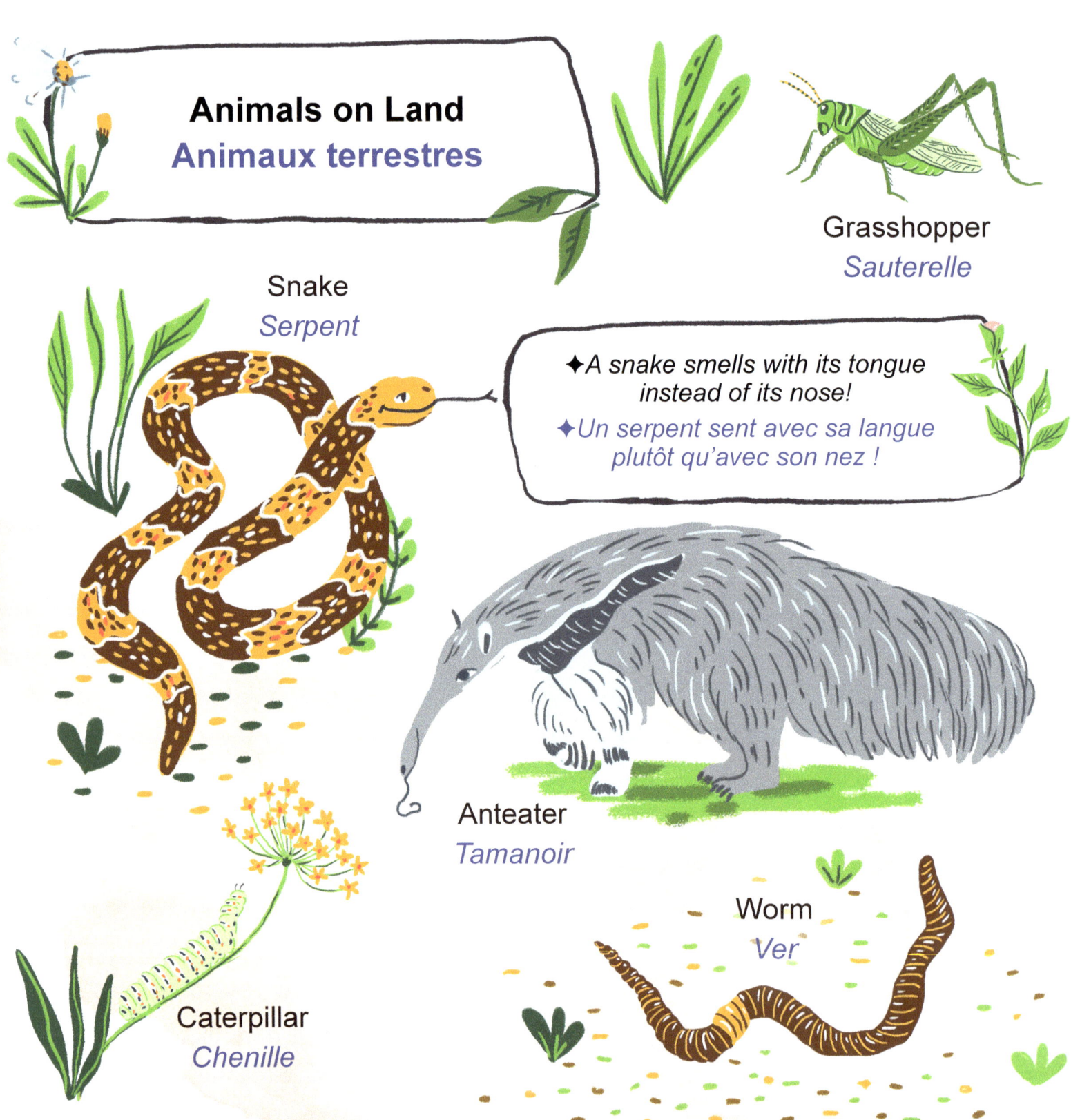

Badger
Blaireau

Porcupine
Porc-épic

Groundhog
Marmotte

✦A lizard can grow a new tail if it loses one!
✦*Un lézard peut faire repousser sa queue s'il la perd !*

Lizard
Lézard

Ant
Fourmi

Small Animals
Petits animaux

Chameleon
Caméléon

Spider
Araignée

♦ An ostrich is the biggest bird, but it cannot fly!
♦ *L'autruche est le plus grand oiseau, mais elle ne peut pas voler !*

Bee
Abeille

♦ A snail carries its home on its back and moves very slowly.
♦ *Un escargot porte sa maison sur son dos et se déplace très lentement.*

Snail
Escargot

Mouse
Souris

Quiet Animals
Animaux silencieux

Turtle
Tortue

Ladybug
Coccinelle

✦ *A turtle can live both on land and in water.*
✦ *Une tortue peut vivre sur terre et dans l'eau.*

Fish
Poisson

Lizard
Lézard

Owl
Hibou

Bat
Chauve-souris

✦ An owl hunts at night and uses its hearing to find food!
✦ Un hibou chasse la nuit et utilise son ouïe pour trouver sa nourriture !

✦ A firefly glows at night to find other fireflies.
✦ Une luciole brille la nuit pour trouver d'autres lucioles.

Raccoon
Raton laveur

Tarantula
Mygale

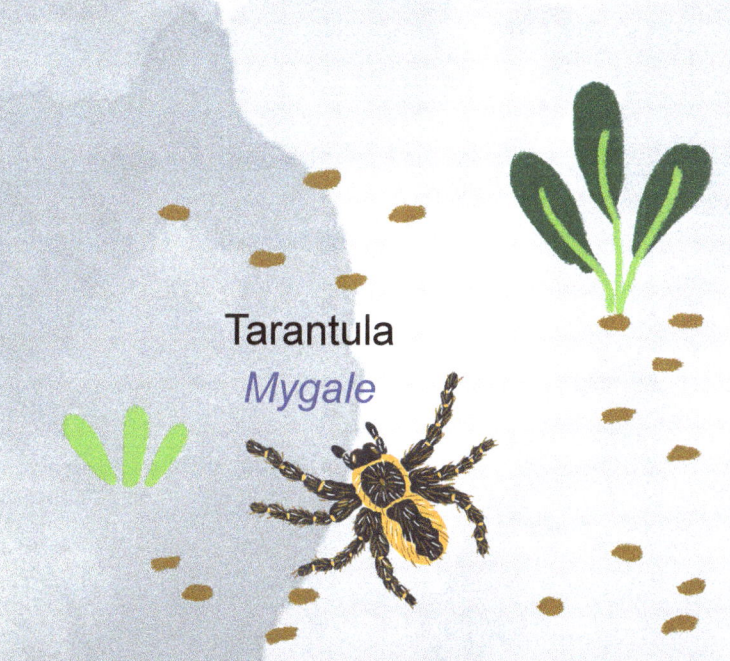

Colorful Animals
Animaux colorés

A flamingo is pink
Le flamant est rose

An owl is brown
Le hibou est marron

A swan is white
Le cygne est blanc

An octopus is purple
Le poulpe est violet

A frog is green
La grenouille est verte

✦ A frog is green, so it can hide among the leaves.
✦ *La grenouille est verte pour se cacher parmi les feuilles.*

Animals and Their Babies
Animaux et leurs petits

Cow and Calf
Vache et Veau

Cat and Kitten
Chat et Chaton

✦ A chick talks to its mother even before it hatches.
✦ *Un poussin parle à sa mère même avant d'éclore.*

Chicken and Chick
Poule et Poussin

Dog and Puppy
Chien et Chiot

Butterfly and Caterpillar
Papillon et Chenille

Sheep and Lamb
Mouton et Agneau

Horse and Foal
Cheval et Poulain

Pig and Piglet
Cochon et Porcelet

Goat and Kid
Chèvre et Chevreau

www.ingramcontent.com/pod-product-compliance
Lightning Source LLC
LaVergne TN
LVHW072056060526
838200LV00061B/4751